GLOVE MONEY

Glore

Sophia

Honey

NIGHTBOAT BOOKS / NEW YORK

Darlin

Printed in the United States

ISBN: 978-1-643-62292-7

Cover art: "Isle of Lesbos II" by Emily Harter, 2020.
Gouche and pencil on paper. Courtesy of the artist.

Design and typesetting by Kit Schluter
Typeset in Sabon LT Pro

Cataloging-in-publication data is available
from the Library of Congress

Nightboat Books
New York
www.nightboat.org

the one with violets in her lap
]mostly
]goes astray

—SAPPHO, *trans. Anne Carson*

CONTENTS

GLOVE MONEY

GLOVE MONEY

I need money to buy gloves
so that I never need again to touch it,
money. I need gloves to separate my hands
from dollars. Also from other hands
when they hand me money, handling
others' money, others' hands,
disgusting. And cold, or hot, and lotion.
To regulate mine own hands' temperatures,
gloves. To buy them, money.

What would be most ideal
would be to have the gloves already.
Somebody, I need you to hand
me some gloves, to hand me
some money there in the glovestore,
so I may hand that money in my glove
to the cashier there, whose name
is French for "casher" and she
will handle me the coins I'll catch
in my leather palm. Or velvet palm,
or artificial breathable fibers
like Lance Armstrong, an athlete of my time.
I would like enough money for gloves,
enough gloves for money, and two hid hands
held by my secret skin.

Once before I knew I was a kind of
lesbian, when I just liked boys, when I was but
a board, I mean when I despised my own thin
smallboned chest, I saw on her,
we were in somebody's driveway,

in full sun, a classmate wore
a hand, a little charm on a chain,
palm-down penny-length ornament
that rested past her clavicle,
above her breasts. It is the part I now
know I love to touch the best, just
where the fat starts. I stood though
dumbstruck, not knowing, not knowing yet
that I am a hand and my sex
is a hand. I thought how erotic,
how could it be so erotic, how secret
that her necklace touches her, she wears the touch
in public.

LIFE STUFF

obviously I am a child of language, for I think I am a child of nature
raised on words I believe I was raised in a green pasture
having ideas about goats, ideas about sheep
yet literally never in my life having been beside a sheep of any color
temperament or texture, sure though of its woolly heft and fecal odor

I think I will lie down in a field with a young man when I am older
I think it's done side by side and facing fondly
the man puts his hand on the woman's wimple and she wettens
they both keep their pretty boots on and wind knits them
with petting grasses, makes of them the nest the infant crawls from

surely I'm a city poet for I think it's done in dusty hay bales
yet have attended field trips and it wasn't sexy
yet have caught heat loping in the easy business of bigger cities
in the building shadow, in the crooks of simple strangers
feel myself most in heat here in this distance that we cultivate together

breathe the most airy here when I'm alone a whole city by me
keeping loose track of who's asleep and who's on running trolleys
if an animal comes near me it's a metaphor for something
if just perhaps my lack of ishness with a larger nature
I do grieve this green earth I'm told is dying, I do grieve the bird names

flying out of use, do blame the warm airports and hot dollars
the vacant rooms stacked high over the city's floorboards
stacked above cardboard signs for money or against fascists
not high above the city's useful streets I slink against a stranger
I am for strangers, nature, myself and strangers

HEY HIVEBODY,

a couple's a wonderful example of a brain
its parts, but just one person I think
just one person speaking alone
has less than half a mind this I believe
and if you want to see a whole body

my angel look to a group of friends
with much sex between them, ordering
drinks swirling from bar to table
stools to outside with cigarettes

and if something has died in you
your humor or your memory of desire
what it was like to broadly want
the joy of drinking that is gone
the trust that you are loved
or that your love is good

then to be with your friends in conversation
is to crowd into a body again
a full mind and participate in it
in what you are missing for instance
desire always very present in a group
ordering drinks on Saturday after the reading
everyone's knees everyone's jacket
reach over you for that

across the deep circle of the table
the couple makes eyes and knows it's time
it's time there is no watch like a couple

if you want to see an entire clock face
please direct your eyes to the couple's eyes
telling each other the time

MFA OR NYC OR FATE

I moved to the Midwest to die
as if it were somehow easier there
or to exit a dark bar of friends
lie down on a sloping lawn
and dissolve there, and wake up a dew
I thought I'd give it a try

I thought booze would open a green portal
I thought the field happened around me
so the sky could join my fears
I thought I'd grow my hair. I fucked

the sidewalk and the grad lounge
and the graveyard and I stuck
Sex trapped me in my form
My formal lover kept the shears
Not the field happened to me but the sheep
Not the shepherd lying down to cum
like I'd wanted and planned

I moved to the Midwest and was a sheep
and was a stalk of corn stuck in the shape
My shepherd stole my hair
My barber harvested my hair
Some movement in me died
some ease, some grass

RIVERR PONDR LAKER SEAR

still bruised from deathgrip
when I cook and when I bake
and when I send emails to a group
and when I send emails to myself
I think I have only myself to remind me
in fact the habit of my own mind is pleasing
pleasure is also bruised
I come sore my immaculate waters
run drawing out these previous waters
I wish rivers of cum didn't all connect
but glad you can't step in it twice
the water's always changing
always flowing oh my heart's a bruise
my clit is a bruise

A TRUE ACCOUNT

At night the heater woke me up
"Are you up?" I was liquescent
runny where my arms
lay along my body, broth
where my legs touch, damp at the
brow, in agitated night
the space heater spoke "Are you
okay?" "I'm hot" I said "Space
heater why are you on, why
are you up so late?"

"You were careless with me,
you didn't press the button, I'm just
doing what I do" "You're
giving me nightmares" I said, "In
my dreams I'm at the start
of laughing opening my mouth
I realize the water's coming in
and begin drowning," "Oof" said
the heater sympathetic while in

the dark the leaning mirror played
steam rising from my hair
"Why are you steaming" "I don't know
you tell me, you're the heat source"
"Honestly I just transmit" it said
"I don't know—something there is
that loves me in this wall?" "That's not
O'Hara" I said "it's Frost anyway I'm

Sappho, or I'm going to be. So
do you have a message for me

am I special to you should I persist
have you visited me tonight to urge me on?"
"Not really" said the heater "I've been here
Hannah ordered me for you" it's true
in horror when she visited and saw
I could not stir to warm myself. "You
didn't shut me off. I don't

know what you do! You shiver on this
pad, you entertain with sex or tales of
woe, you call our room your
Garret of Despair. I mean you
heat it some but slowly,
no offense, honestly I can't tell what
your function is, this isn't
critical, I came here in a box"
sultry on the mattress

I shifted to gaze back, "Heater,
I don't know, I transmit too maybe
but I'm never sure quite what, to
be candid, you're right
I'm not much of a heater" "That's
not what I mean, I'd never
compare you and I, for all I know
you're a fridge" "True" I
nodded in the dark "I'll shut
you off now if you'd like" "That's fine,

but do it for yourself. I don't mind
in fact I can't" Space heater
what else is there to heat but

space I thought, gaping the sheets
to vent a wave of steam.
"Goodnight heater" "Sophie,
goodnight. And don't feel bad" "I won't
heater" I said, "Thank you" "You're
welcome" it said. Coolly.

SHE'S GOT A HABIT

Tonight I like cooking again. I'd thought
that taken from me but I
persist in my design, I like
making mistakes
and eating them.

Refine my errors in the pan.
My skillset. I sing
"You're going to lose that girl" and I am
John Lennon. I'm that girl.
I'm the schmuck receiving warning,

and I'm the predatory lesbian
promising oral understanding to
the girls at karaoke.
But I'm unbelievable,
I croon to him
"You'll be the lonely one" and I mean

me, the dizzy cook, who bites
the tops off
carrots, swaps recipes mid-
bake, spits in the pan
to check the oil's hot. And sings
to the gnarly pot liquor "Identity

can't be concise" that's Lisa
Robertson, "It's knit from sequins
lust and scatters" lineation mine
I think she means knit
as in "the Stuff of life to knit me blew
hither and here am I" that's Housman.

Because knitting is concision,
whether wind
or poets do it. But of disparate
stuff, it's true, "of life" "of decorations"
being a queer and
being alone or dating

a man, the kind of man who
mostly dates queer women. I'm
editing my dinner
as I eat, I put Robertson's "and"
in the Housman. It's a lot to be

the first to call yourself
she or not, the only one
to call yourself I. I wrote a friend
"Your name drifts in the rising
conversation/ at times a toy,
at times a weapon," and
most solemnly I meant it.

The first *She's Gotta Have It*
showed a woman who "defied convention"
nonverbally, by doing
what she likes. In the remake
she reposes in
her niche and self declares "sex-positive
polyamorous pansexual" and
the criticks howled against our age,

against the knitting of her name.
No edge! No raw, no fecklessness

no lack of self-consciousness!
I see their grief,

but I do not feel their grief.
Not as I eat.
Not as the wind of the past three years
sous cheffing to a tyrant
whines at the window. When I
named it, to name
did fuck me up

and it did unfuck me up. I wrote
a poem: *Divination*

> some things feel like harm
> but aren't
>
> but can be
> if identified as such
>
> in fact
> all things can be harm
> if felt as harm
> and identified as harm
> and not disidentified
>
> that is
> all things
> named harm
> if allowed to stay thus named
> may
> harm

and some harms
left unnamed
of course
compound

or can be largely cured
by naming
as a ham
by salt
can

some things feel like chicken parm
but aren't
and cannot be
though named
though felt as chicken parm
cannot be
aren't

rename it
be it damage or a sandwich
now ask
is it still harm?
is it still parm?

if it's still parm
then you can eat it all
right up
it will not harm you

if it's hot
it might
so

touch the parm
is it harmful?

if it is
it's harm
now wait
now call it warm

I was thinking, I think, about the ways
naming a crisis
resets one's instrument. Once

aware of mistreatment, I
suffered, a while, in a way
my lack of notice had delayed.
After the fact, after
the fact was named. And for some time
I saw harm everywhere. Though

I do not see it eating meat.
This is likely dissociation. Like
changing the subject. Or rhyme.

Rhyme is a way of leaping
out of your head into the world.

COW LONELY ARE YOU?

on the internet of wildflowers
a white flower
is not what I see
blue furling dress petal
a flower is part dress part animal
part vegetable part face
an internet a lighted
shape of light on screen

in the floral city at the flower's center
chrysanthemum
lily or amaranth a bristling civic center

halated pistils
furry filament
when you, a flower, are asked for poppies'
whereabouts by vegan panthers
don't anther

pick the flowers
take their part
they are part part part petal
scintillant on hilltops
hosting an air
a fertile bee-provoking glitch
part dream, part snack, a culture

CHOSEN FAMILY

> *"But I want more out of life than an extended family of ex-lovers"*
> —ALISON BECHDEL, self-portrait, speech bubble

but I do not want much more than an extended family of ex-lovers
but I do want a love or more to share with me my mattress
but want a new person to start in my body and extend
but I do want to extend my family out of my body and alive
but I want my ex-lovers to come back as lovers sometimes
but I want love to loop

but I do want much more than an extended family of ex-lovers
I want more than an extended family of ex-lovers wants
I want more than the families extending from the families of my
  ex-lovers and their ex-lovers and the families of their ex-lovers and
  all the desire it takes to create families of ex-lovers or new persons
  extending
more than all their wants I want
just one extensive love

but I do want more than a distended farm hilly of maneuvers
I do want more than a suspended flan milling in my œuvre
I'd like to extend to you my familiarity with others
what I want butts heads with my wants' knees under the covers
mothers druthers hovers butters
I want nothing more than an intended lamb filly pho eggs l'œufs roofs
I want to learn French, I hear it is the language of love

BUSINESS

for Bebe

My nose is incisive. I nose
what to do and does it. Yet mouthe
endless mealy queries
always never biting always simper
try to get a clear cut till I drool

yet my nose knows what to do.
My nose gives good nose.
I give good nose forward to the air,
pose a hard profile, make a point.
My face is a cloud! My face is a chord!
My face brings feeling to the phone!
It busies the phone line with tugs
sighs and hovers at the touch
the taunt of a freely floating hand

but that nose, though! Crisply!
You can lead me by the tit,
you can get big hands in my belly
my belly is wool! Dirty wool outdoors!
You can pry my legs they are clockwork
clock and unclock, you can guess
my legs' rotations and anticipate
their halt. My head faints
easily with a little heat
and height. My palms are slick

not with sweat but what
I've grabbed, fistfuls of coconut

squeezed into butter, if you wrap me up
I can't slip away, and you can hook
a hand in my cunt and keep me,
can't you, though
you can't grab
my nose. My nose will look at you.
Gets what you do, it will not

falter in its condemnation. Brisk nose,
bright gate! My eyes are scum
limpid on the superficial face,
my wanton neck is just the size of hands,
if the hands know what they want.
But up front my nose abstains.
You can't take it.

GOOD NATURE

Something there is that does not love a wallet
but it is not my coy dollar

a penny's halved she sighs
a penny's yearned
a penny salved
will slip from your budget

there are ways my neighbor understands me
better than I and I am these trees
and yet my sight's clouded with leaves
roughed o'er with bark

from the inlet of my neighbor's understanding
comes my name at me

purchasing foothold on my clay ways
my property that is my deep body
or her corolla

the little dollar spoons my wallet's folds
and spooned again by my wallet's outer folds
feels valuable in leather

buttered penny
dry dollar in the wallet
my friendship budgeted and bound
I lie on my side of the property line and I'm
you don't cross me

I LIKE YOU'RE PUTTING A LOT ON ME

Some friends joined me today
at lunch break at the duck pond
Ah. Your friends are ducks.
Your friendship, bread.
Ah, what is mine. Receptive
listening? Egregious hugs?
An overlapping mucilage
or lightly watered
free-growing frisson? My tendency
to squeal at what you say you
bad beast? How I confess
at the drop of a foot
just how that foot has made me
feel? How I feel all my thoughts
and offer them to you
in handled wads?
Mama said
you are adept
at making friends
in every situation.

I make them out of bread.
No but some bakers do.
I build a bear
but that's no fun
I want the bear to come to me
I want a part
of me I'm not
looking at to lure you

helpless I want not
to be self known just but

brought by love
to light!

Out the duck pond
a lady of the lake
extrudes her arm,
offers this sword

and I say
some of my best friends
unspool gradually!

I LIKE ANYTHING

You thought a plate had landed
on your table
but I placed it

I brought this clover
to the field
Haven't tried it,
hear it's sweet

Would you like more
soda in your life?
Would you like bright
water in your glass?

Black legged bee
Dry bladed grassy patch
Would you like more
spring feeling?

Would you like some
sitting in a day and you really
do what you're doing?

Not always seeking
the ledge of attention
with your shod
your insensible feet

Would you like anything!

The bee paws the petals
dabs the pancake
I like this insane music,

heels of the poets
in the clover

the inhabited flavor
of a juice called nectar

Anything! Anything!
Anything!

THAT'S MY WEAKNESS NOW

I'm well known throughout the co-ops for being a splashy dishwasher,
and I'm well known in the suburbs for singing to the mayor's daughter.

Wine is cheaper than books unless you drink it by the bowlful.
I read books hand over hand and my hands are soulful.

Softer than a cloud in a child's rhyme, your dainty cleaning after love.
Softer than the edges of a fan's blades furred with dust.

You speak intimate universes to your listeners, then make moue.
Surely no one since Boop has winced at fierier triumphs than Sophia.

BEING THERE IN FIVE

for BB

you've been waiting for me in the bar
the natural bar where the wine smells like horseshit
the white wine basks in the glass
when you drink it it laughs
effervescent

I come in late but really fast
as if I cannot bear
your wait my pained face sings
singes me wounded I fucked up
wrong bus my co-op for my horse my cart
I came on foot I slipped on cum
I am tardy and I love you the better for it

I forgive you you say
I still want to see you you say
your grace finishes us both

nailpolishes the hoof to a horseshoe
I shod a girl I said I
riddled her with my intentions
you want to have a baby?
you want to be my daughter?
I rode her back to the pasture
and her body to the water
What are you drinking?
Just you say The house red

It's good you say lightly the push on *it's*
I'll have it too You look beautiful

you have to deal with my compliments
you grind a little your teeth in your chair
you thank me

Who is this girl you ask
The magnetic one who taps
a bottle cap to her temple and it stays? No I say
She only wished to be my anecdote Is it the one
you think is dangerously young? No oh no
she is younger than that

OH BRANDON I yell REMEMBER
everyone twists in their wooden chair
Why do bars have to be so quality I ask you Why
must this field of daisies so closely attend

What Sophia What are you asking you ask me
your mouth an ordinary distance from the window

no one who sees us would guess I hear
the clink of every marble in my sack and feel
breathed by the air a waft of blousey silk and that
as you modestly describe the ancientest
language you've learned I ride

the rolling gestures of your hands
all horselike, and arrive

SAPPHO AS QUANTUM BRACKET

How will I write Sapphic poetry
for though I am a woman, loving women
my love is a man's!
A man's solicitous desire! I scratch my throat.
My voice goes husky as I say your name,
I measure the yard with a footlong hotdog,
but I fuck up the numbers
because the sausage softly bends
and I get distracted
pressing it against the exterior molding.
My love was invented to secure our infant housing
and every time we touch
I want to write a check.
Not necessarily to you, but somebody.
I am so dumb. I am so lucky.
I am certain I am overlooking my uselessness.

None of this is true!
My love is a fruit!
I am just like Sappho, bearing your loss
to a wedding. And I am assured
of my uselessness, here
is its catalogue. The yard is trees
a long lap of trees across a woody forest!
Peeling down the sea!
And I am speaking to you
in this group of our peers
yearning, and I know my yearning is sonorous!

Because I am not trying to take you from anybody.
If you want to go

all I can do is sing you hotly.
So that you will look for me when your water breaks.
When birth pain takes you out,
you'll feel my face in darkness.
When you hear your name, elsewhere
my voice will sing it lightly under.

[You'll name your baby Sophaikos]

[The fruit of my invention seeds its sugar in your dreams.]

GODS PEED

I take a lot of pleasure in this moment

I am in bed eating macaroni
[ ] is on her way to the show
she is working the bar

and it's a vale of tears outdoors
gods peed I said to her
she caught the pause

gods' pee and tears available to us
tonight
we grieve and feel relief

I loved having her come over
a surprise
loved fucking her in the rain sound
while the cars move past it
and the youtube wails

she and I crack up
but I touch her face
grieve as I roll my hand across her

lesbians love to fuck sadly
straights love it grimly
like they were farming

maybe what I find tragic is that she is young
and so beautiful

I will follow her to the show at 11:39 pm
I will be a little in her way
as she opens beers

all of this sounds so beyond the grave to me
that's what it is

I am feeling the loss of this beautiful night
drying up in the sun

my mac and cheese losing its heat
the soft rain drying

[AND]

the draped plant also wears
its hair to the left

I have never been so sensible
to long hair on a woman

I have never been so hurt
by long hair on the left

when you wind your rivulet
to the side

and show your neck
I look at it

SAPPHIC LOOP

Don't you feel how much give is in me
when I reach for your name in my phone
   I hold down
everything else in the room rising.
      My mind's a busy pond.
  My kitchen is the bread's bedroom.
I own so little furniture, would knock it to the floor
   if you were calling.
And I'd stand on top of the parking structure
    seeking your sign!
In narrow clouds endored in sunset door,
in my new phone's yearning for its service,
in immovable concrete sleek like seals,
      the red crease where my fingers join
    I'm leaning for
              any sense that you might need me.
Sappho probably went to the beach.
Where are her shorelines, her waves,
  their colors?
Was the ocean dark like apples,
did the apples cloud her bowl? I have no art in me,
  no nature.
My poems talk and talk.
I hurt my back yet lift you to pin
    you against the kitchen wall
           I risk it
        desire to
          you say thank you
   the room rises.
Why are you subsisting without me
    my friends? Do not

demand me, my lover, who could be
  my lover?
Don’t you feel how much give is in me (*repeat from top*)

FLAGRANCE OF SAPPHO

I don't know what I want
tonight, knowing I want
to see her.

AT THE CHANGI AIRPORT

on a green lips-shaped loveseat
between two trees rooted below the floor
I see mist and I learn the ceiling is misting
a rain and air barely appearing down
on my library book, my open face phone
I am thinking of a friend's beautiful, biting eyes
and inexpert kissing he effects
not with his lips but with his mandibles
I'm eating ham toast from Paris Baguette
the cheese is on top of the top slice of bread
only the ham is sandwiched
so everything is a mouth here
the Changi airport cradling me
salivarily between crystal windows
a little person trying to live in a giant
a little person trying to live in money
the tooth has a door if I am very lucky
the tooth has a chimney like a memory of housing
child artists in the hottest suburbs of SoCal
know home is hearth and smoke toodles out
a red rectangle and grass greens the front patch
a narrow blue sky hovers high above
a mother, a father, a sister, a brother
a family dog, a family cat, an associated bird
and where the neighbors the traffic the wild
and the abandoned live is just white
between where the green
lip and blue lip of lawn and sky part

L'OVERMIND

No I understand nothing
H.D says overmind is a cap
a hovering cap around the head

distorting sight and its tentacles wave
down through and around and
energy wells
in the hands and belly and cunt

Out my head a beam of light
traces a triangle between me
(my heart) and you (your heart)
and lamp (its bulb)

I see swimming inside the triangle
flashing red then blue, then
a pulse eats itself up and in
the devoured space
a relief of fluttering palms displays

the complete life cycle of a swan
blank egg to swan
full swan that beats
its whiteout wings

I know nothing of the heart
I know nothing of your needs

I don't know if I'm someone a woman could love
My housemate said women don't want
to date us because they see us
men are satisfied with just pleasing us

but my therapist said that was unexamined
so I'm drawing a shape in the air
for the image of myself already
embroidered in love and feathered although

I see your eyes and I see them narrow
I feel more held by your skepticism
than I do by anyone's desire
I don't know what to do about it

Do swans die of a broken heart?
Can a swan break your arm with its neck?
Do Swans sing before they die?
How do you get rid of a swan?

WATERING

I slide glass along a superficial lake
to match myself to surface tension

I mean to twin

I lip the water's
waver with my

lower lip and
water hovers

limp in my mouth and then it drains

and my shoulders and
my elbows and

my wingèd knees abundantly
dent the waves the waves

the little waves has a lake

a balancing of glass
mine lens

against its wetted clarity it runs
water against it

over a waver
a hand snakes up

an elbow frogs

below in green lake water
that limply plucked is clear

see sky

see the nebulous knees of your lover
she is in the water

alone and tries to match its mirror

oh lover blink water [against/into]
the infinite fringe of your eyes

STAR ASTRINGENT

when there's an aching in me
can you gentle it

it can't be cleaned
I don't need vinegar

I don't need water,
vinegar, or a puncture

well maybe a lavender
maybe a needle bed

gong struck within
the ground where I stand

to head giddy up me
to let out a sob to outswim me

so there's water without me
water against me

in the distance white vinegar burns
is awakening

maybe [   ]
so perilous [   ]

you remove nail polish
from your toes up against

my open windowsill
so no matter how close I come I'm across the room

and I want to be just eyes
just water lightly held

but when I feel the organ of my heart
tighten and harm me

then I want my body clutched by denim exactly
and I can ask for more

will you steady the bedframe
will you when there's an earthquake

as there was last night and the night before
and is coming for us

hold me with your arm around me?
will you stand behind me and hold me?

BROOKE OFFERS THE DOLL OF HERSELF

Brooke who looks like a dahlia
brought me a bouquet of dahlias
so now I can see how she looks
with her white-green wisps of hair
a dahlia is not separate from its stem
not from the green process of forming
a plant that does not fully ripen
the dahlia smells sweet and green
its head heavy like Brooke's head is
round skulled and little nosed
and pink in the petal's vulvar folds
each dahlia a full
blown garden in the wind
or a swell of roomies in Oakland
liberating land from the lords
Brooke is tall and long stemmed
and in that she is just a dahlia
who would bring me herself

She budgets for wild caught fish and berries
like a bear would if it were a dahlia
and I love her very much today
if I had a vase that was clear enough
I'd place in it some leavings of my love

SAPPHO IN SAG

as a Leo sun, I am large
and as a Gemini rising, I contain
multitudes. I can't think of a single line
of poetry about the moon. Luna
I think Lorca would say, and it would mean
woman, shadow, death,
fuck the Falange. Good point,
the moon, and the stars?
Don't tell me the stars have pictures
who we are, and we're holding hands.
As a Libra Moon, I'd like
to be with you forever

in argument. I am I or am she,
love from kneejerk
come up with the sun from the sea.
My gravity, my gracious. The heater vent's
under my mattress and I have a hot
mattress. As a Leo sun. And I like
losing you in the crowd. I like
pushing through to find you, and when you find
me or when I didn't know you would
but you're here and say my name
I really like to come as I am.

TOURISM

I'm going to travel through the dark
to 1959 to lick
Diane di Prima's feet that toe
the lid of the white-washed piano
as she reads from her first book
This Kind of Bird Flies Backward
in a bar called Gaslight

all the Beats sit around little tables

she's set herself on the piano's head
and toes its lap

I want to hear
the music of her feet

that are bare to me
laced by gladiator flats
to her mid-calf

One flat's ties fell
rest at her ankle
I will adjust it for her
while she turns the page

while she reads to her lovers
and theirs
Amiri Baraka (here LeRoi Jones)
Hettie Jones

her hair she calls crewcut

to my eye is feminine, folded
even in a cracked black and white old photo

could be gripped
and her round ankles

SAPPHIC 13

friend
to speak to you directly

no I don't feel a soul in any rose
not in my body either

nor do I believe
a heaven awaits

instead the delicate layers of me
drink time

not like a rose

do not in dew at 5am
all lipped by crystals sink
red petals into morning

a rose is a rose body

into the white breath of your scarf
here you are in New York City

I would like you to live

your hurt heart your hurt heart
Sappho had friends

a rose's color isn't soul
nor is a petal's feeling

rose is what rose does
in the English language

GRATITUDE IS COUNTERREVOLUTIONARY

yes bite the hand
it should not hold the food
suspended so your throat's
tight so your neck's
bent back in feeding

why not place food on your floor periphery
back away and let you eat
food as food

if it needs its palm licked
let it ask for that
offer a palm
not lunch

this is very Diane di Prima don't you think

eat the hand that feeds you
then—what would she say—plant your own kibble

REVOLUTIONARY FRAGMENT

There's not going to be
standardized gay vocabulary
unless we all lose

SAPPHIC LECTURE

if you fear you are not gay enough
go out and do something about it
like suck a dyke's dick
or get fisted
dump your boyfriend
fear can be destructive and it will age you
it will age you like the sun
but you can enjoy your fear if you are careless with it
you can enjoy the sun
and let it graze upon your baby skin

if you fear not being queer enough
try to think of yourself as lyrical dirt
anticapitalist animals might furrow
sunlight might lavish sex upon
notice yourself mobile
[a bouncing part of the natural world]

if you fear not being read as queer
cut your hair weird
quit a job
practice your art
or I don't know join a cell
locate a clit

I am trying to show you how good this can be
how much joy like how much liquid in these clouds
men can be wonderful but too many will ruin your life
they will ruin the garden of your love
because they will stand around you like a fence and crowd out
the queer birds, the queer beasts
and the queer creatures of the forest's fucking

BI ERASER

It's more lesbian culture to be bi
than lesbian. Sappho married a man
no that was rumors.
Still, wouldn't it be lesbian
to marry a man and all your friends
sulk about it and write poems? Sappho
would write you a poem.

There are two kinds of lesbian: Sappho,
and a roomful of lesbians. A lesbian couple
falls into one or the
other of those categories. Violet and I are Sappho.
You and I are a roomful of lesbians. Brooke
keeps dating men but she does it
in a really gay way, she keeps
picking them up in
trucks, she calls them
"boys." Men like her so much they
pant, they get all relaxed and wet. I guess
if you really really
really like men it's not even
heterosexual it's just nice, right? Easy.
And I love her. Sappho
loves women. A roomful of lesbians
only loves a roomful of lesbians.

When I'm with a man I'm never gloating
never think oh all the lesbians must be sad. I just
get like, oh no, they won't
let me in the room, the roomful
of lesbians! Let me in! I said the thing about

lesbian culture being bi and Ronah
was pissed, she wants credit for
her dedication. When Rowan got gay he said
he was gayer than me and I
was like put in the *hours* bitch.
Did you know Psappho spelled it Psappho.
Psopphie. Did you know they called her
"violet-haired"

SAPPHIC SALT

I press my hand
into wet sand
a soft mouth traps it

waves
lap my wrist
but that's extra

and pressing winds
press of similar
skin

the unspoilt line of
I

sworn defender
of girl on girl island

I wrote this verse
to fight with a friend
who kept hanging dykes
from clits like clothespins

Let go of your terf shit,
glukumelon. You somehow know
she wouldn't stroke

dick silk of a surfacing
jellyfish bulb with those
lyrical hands?

No poet's real, no
only our need for our
own need's ancientness
sucks in the sand

TRICK SAPPHICS

astrology
doesn't interest me
altogether anymore till
your prehensile saturn
intersects
w/mine
in June
all things are dear

CUP GLASS

Women will always have shoulders
they won't always be women
        they'll have shoulders

Beloveds will always

turning a shoulder
before light of when that
breaks through what

drink water from a seen-through cylinder
        her shape a shape against
A beloved will turn
        water from her shoulder

        Why do I like to be across the room

I am sick with love
it has spoilt my pleasure
I do not want to travel
or cast a shadow
        I do not want to summer in the city

I only want each day to sign
the possibility of her arrival
like a tanned edge of toast
signifies crispness

LAMBIENCE

I try each peach pear plum
only plum pear impeachably
fruit reaches my tongue
youth is about being juicy
trying is the wiring of the tree
the twig is sticky

I can break each unbearable fruit
off a branch and if my hand wants to give
my hand a gift
it crushes it

some hells naturally occur
some heavens are free forming
some heaven is inherent

INVOCATION

o Aphrodite
make her love me
even though she is focusing

I INSIST HER EYES ARE STARS

they are blue and gray not unfiltered spectrum
        they are languishing
bathed in tear slime not fiery
nonetheless   her eyes are stars

it is obvious   her eyes are stars
her eyes are stars   I cannot touch them
I am not permitted to hurt her
I am forbidden by my desire not   to hurt her

so too am I forbidden star caress
                distance forbids
so too by my desire   for I would survive
to touch a star would be to disappear
      so too to be
the sort of person who would touch an eye

not I
so not, in so doing, I

furthermore her eyes break out to infinite points
        are radiantly fringed
furred as the stars by light's outstretching arc
                        by light as I receive their sight down here
                her eyes that I receive in mine
                    look into me and through

they are not, like the stars, what loves
        her love, my love, and all love refracts
through and to her starlike eyes

SAPPHIC TROUBADOUR

She is always willingly appearing womanly
and I love to tease her for her long thighs

for not wanting what she's wont to want
for forbidding herself dew of her dawning

But now I am what she forbids herself
because I misbehaved on that bridge!

And I really don't think she took it well
when I tried to lift her skirt when she was talking

SAPPHIC SAPPHIC FOR VIOLET

My pussy sucking yours

NATCH'S GREEN FIST IS GOALS

Lovely a tree smell, a lovely lion's fur
once you see lion you can't stop
seeing it, lion fur, gold lion.
Her mane, her land of lambs, her
eating sunflower hair, her seeded
eyes. You wanna go? I wanna. The eye
wants, the eyes wanna. It was a soft
fitted shirt, her hips, not
her stride, her long legged, impatient,
the hem narrow, amazing its rigidity,
amazing she had to stride with one hand
holding up her skirt, people
peopling the green could see
her knees, impatient stride, lift
hem to move knees onward,
the field lies flat to be taken,
our, my room running in place on a flat
lawn, a rich green, a ghost goes through,
make like a wall and let it
pass through you, let the gods depend
on your skin. Go let them
be. Only a human is a
trespasser. I'm gonna, I intend, I wanna gonna
clamber into a chamber. Life's the kiss
of death. You're the end
of me, the start. An alive
light spiral, no if it's light it spreads,
it does not bottle, cup, nor brim.
It does not remain, an energy
expends. Though a tree's not spent
in smelling. Go there at once
sharing the abundance of three.
You try. A special try.

WHEN YOU KNOW

you know
when you have your love and it casts a little shadow
like a vase moved against the light cast by the window
the window's sun it performs against the vase's figure
its element of darkness

when your love you know is moved by a hand and stains
the page stains thus a movement caught by volcano
asked against a blond wallpaper
a movement

when you know your love has flowed
it went left and left a trail like a beard
a remaining trail that says the words have flown
left like hand shadows of birds fly in the winter

O LIKE A MERMAID'S HEART

O like a mermaid's heart
breaks and she is seafoam
of the sea her body parts in
in waves as in ambient waffle
love's butter breaks in flower

ALAS GLEANER

Always watering the greener grass. In my neighbor's lawn,
idealesque. The far bank of your lawn, where I project
myself. I photograph my watering, its rainbows, light
litter and spinning in clean air above our grasses,
yours and mine. My grasses stand not on my lawn but lie
and writhe, for it is hard there, dry
and gold. Where is your

lawn my sweetheart asks, new, sentimental, ready to
relax, barefoot, her shoes in hand, the sidewalk wet
beneath her ready feet. Isn't that one
yours, she asks, she lifts her foot to point its toes
at your amaranth bergamot calla lily dogwood
eyewhite freesia gladiolas hollyhocks impares
jasper kindred spirits lilac manzanita naked ladies
oleander poppyseed quince rosemary spruce
trappelpan umbrella leaf viridium
willow xantharose yarrow
and zinnias abundantly tousled in the spray
of my endless hydrating hose.

LIKE VIOLET

Violet
Violet wishing
I do not tire of you
I tire of days
low in the water
I wish my room were full of
breathing plants
o Violet if
I make of you my room
I won't know how
to keep my
eye on you and my eye
's doing for me
something nutritive

at Woolsey at Tyrone
Steve and Melissa's
reading Ivy
braided your hair
you sat alert
like a fairy snared
a ferret in the snow
I watched, snared too
the gold lamp glow
as your hair beneath
Ivy's quick
hands became
scales and
fins

a
narrow
river and
a bird ahead
soft fishes
vivid in a river
a fragrant opening
of cantaloupe
giveth a wedge
the objects of
my measuring
I see you when
we sleep
you sleep
deep into me so deep
this morning you
were as far from the wall
as my exact body

AN ANSWER

Another poet is an answer
How can I ask my questions
in the shadow of her answer?

When I know a sound is coming
how can I pause?
When I do not set the silence?

On the lip of a hill
in the orange lip of fruit
of the sun passing her extremely slowly

Passing over her and in her like a gaze
a slow gaze of an interested waiter
risking a tip to linger near her table

When it's gone the dirt road
very flat is unapologetic
very laid out in moon

I know an answer's not an end
How can I ask my questions
in the illuminating shadow of
her eyes gathering lashes?

APPEAR OF BODICE

Your form is loitering among the trees
You take the time you want to leave
to anything
Your form is loitering
These downtown Oakland streets I like
These open nights like oceans or Olympic oceans
The open mattress feeling on the floor
I take the place
I can't take time
The sun is buoyed by its sentences
The book is nebulous with real fog
but the fog is generative
it forms

Your form is loitering among the trees
You are the olives grey and green
You are the wine
drunk wine that dries the tongue
above wine's head
the sky's birds masticate what clouds
are throaty closure of
I say, your form is loitering among the trees
it melts the space that ought be cut between
That's not a silhouette
That's a form I can't get to leave the forest

POWER RANGER

my sitting in a floral plane w/ lover neighbor
wishing okay to neighbor strangers
is a way to be even handed
and not spill all the egg jelly at once

walking home I might step in a dog clue
or see the day sink pinkly with a turned head
like neighbor sealing the party door

I hear mention of jealousy like injury
a grating of the skull, genuinely nasty

but I am jealous of all the best people
it's like my invitation to the party

neighbor, to be delicious is okay
my eyes digest what can't my gut
I hold you as an ache

often holding gifts
is how neighbor lover comes
to the door, unnecessarily
like the daylight handing me a candelabra

daylight pockets the candelabra gently
this here was the digression of a dog

why my time is speeding up so suddenly
because I'm not miniature anymore
and my days are just details in a year's mood

I said no more resolutions
just wishes, sibling neighbor
grabbed the birthday candles
and we handed everybody one

and when the New Year was agreed upon
didn't improve

OFT PERMITTED TO JOIN IN AGREEMENT

two legs converged in a hazel wood and I
I let myself be swallowed by
coniference.

GLOW THING

What a day to be me, small amount
of baby's breath, not clover, not moss not
moth not a real baby but the green
small thought of air her mouth
takes in and softly
lets, and I am also
the easy rhythm of these words
Buh buh buh buh
I love earth darkening
I love sky split and
balmy heather, violet
is my favorite, the hue and
girlfriend, at home now, not
rooted in the lovely
dirt rather spread
like young intelligent butter in the bed,
probably writing a poem.

ACKNOWLEDGMENTS AND THANKS:

This book samples shamelessly the phrases and formulations of other authors: Robert Duncan, June Jordan, Barbara Guest, Robert Frost, Alfred Tennyson, A.E. Housman, Diane di Prima, Frank O'Hara, Ogden Nash, Lisa Robertson, Bernart de Ventadorn via Lisa Robertson, Heraclitus via Disney's Pocahontas, and Sappho via Anne Carson.

Earlier versions of these works appeared in *Chicago Review, The Brooklyn Rail, Elderly, Hot Pink, Castle Grayskull, Neck, Send Me Press, Poetry Northwest, F, Kenyon Review, Can We Have Our Ball Back, baest, Spirit Duplicator*, and *Social Text*. Thank you to the editors of these publications.

So many thanks to the dreamboats at Nightboat! What a fantastic crew/fleet. Thank you to my editor Lindsey Boldt for your wizardry at every stage: you understood what worked and didn't, you helped me hear the book of it all under the clangor of my feelings and feelings about those feelings, and you sat on my living room carpet and used your extrasensory perception to arrange this manuscript into its final form. You're so good at this and I'm so lucky for that. Thank you also to Trisha Low, Kit Schluter, Emily Bark Brown, Dante Silva, Lina Bergamini, Morgan Levine, and Stephen Motika for working on this book and for encouraging me at every stage. I demand lots of encouragement even though I will never stop.

Thank you to early readers of this manuscript—Mandy Gutmann-Gonzalez, anise cinquepalmi, Jacob Kahn, Dan Poppick, and Zoe Tuck—

for your wisdom and friendship. Extra thanks to Dan for suggesting I write a poem called "glove money."

I wrote many of these poems in rooms or parks or while conferencing online with the participants in my workshops. Thank you, Passion Vine Academics. Thank you Teen Poet Avengers/Under the Library Press/Dover Park Poetry Grownups. Thank you ongoingly to my brilliant companions in the Generative Poetry Workshops. Writing with you all is a sustaining joy.

My forever thanks to Violet for your several readings, your teasing yet stalwart support, and for letting me love you in public. I love you even more everywhere else.

Sophia Dahlin is a poet in Berkeley, California, where she organizes readings, co-edits Eyelet Press, and teaches generative poetry workshops out of her apartment, nearby parks, and the internet. Her first full length collection, *Natch,* came out in 2020.

NIGHTBOAT BOOKS

Nightboat Books, a nonprofit organization, seeks to develop audiences for writers whose work resists convention and transcends boundaries. We publish books rich with poignancy, intelligence, and risk. Please visit nightboat.org to learn about our titles and how you can support our future publications.

The following individuals have supported the publication of this book. We thank them for their generosity and commitment to the mission of Nightboat Books:

Kazim Ali • Anonymous (4) • Ava Aviva Avnisan • Jean C. Ballantyne • Will Blythe • V. Shannon Clyne • Theodore Cornwell • Ulla Dydo Charitable Fund • Gisela Gamper • Photios Giovanis • Amanda Greenberger • David Groff • Parag Rajendra Khandhar • Katy Lederer • Shari Leinwand • Elizabeth Madans • Ricardo Maldonado • Ethan Mitchell • Caren Motika • Elizabeth Motika • Asker Saeed • The Leslie Scalapino - O Books Fund • Amy Scholder • Thomas Shardlow • Benjamin Taylor • Jerrie Whitfield & Richard Motika • Clay Williams

This book is made possible, in part, by grants from the New York City Department of Cultural Affairs in partnership with the City Council, the New York State Council on the Arts Literature Program, and the Topanga Fund, which is dedicated to promoting the arts and literature of California.

NYC Cultural Affairs NEW YORK STATE OF OPPORTUNITY. Council on the Arts